As A Stock or Thinketh In Its Heart So It Is

Being A Treatise On The Effect Of Thought on the Future Price For Stocks & Commodities.

This is a Companion Text to:
The Book of Impulse
& The Dictionary of (Investment) Thoughts

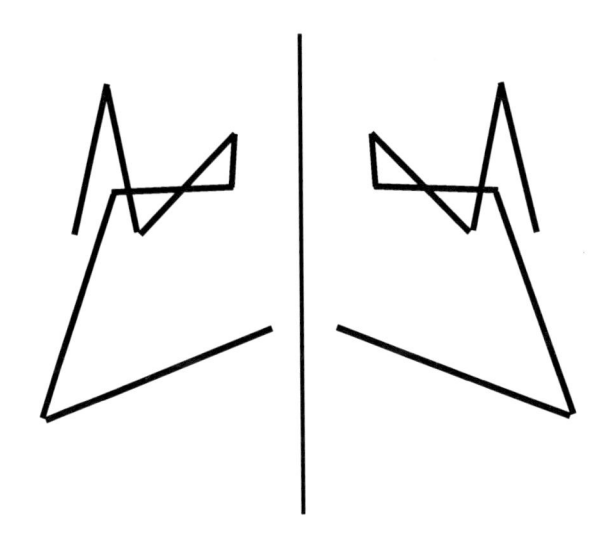

Nsingo Sakala

As A Stock or Commodity
Thinketh In Its Heart So It Is

First Published 2012 by
Nsingo Sakala
52 Mellis Avenue
Kew Riverside
London
TW9 4BD
www.nsingo.com

Copyright © 2012 by Nsingo Sakala
As A Stock or Commodity Thinketh in Its Heart So It Is

ALL RIGHTS RESERVED. This book contains material protected under International and Federal Copyright Laws and Treaties. Any unauthorized reprint or use of this material is prohibited. No part of this book may be reproduced or transmitted in any form or by any means, electronic or mechanical, including photocopying, recording, or by any information storage and retrieval system without express written permission from the Nsingo Sakala. Reviewers may quote brief passages.

ISBN: 978-1-908482-56-3
British Library Cataloguing in Publication Data Available upon request.

Cover and Design by Nsingo Sakala
Typeset in Kew London

Printed in London

The paper used in this publication meets the minimum requirements of the International Standard for Information Sciences.

ISBN 978-1-908482-56-3

iii

**As A Stock or Commodity
Thinketh In Its Heart So It Is**

Dedicated to

James Allen

&

The Scientific Investor.

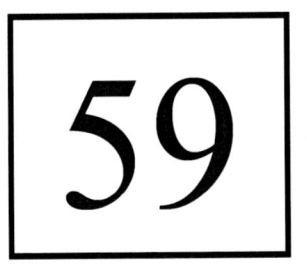

$$\boxed{59}$$

"Train up a child in the way he should go: and when he is old, he will not depart from it."

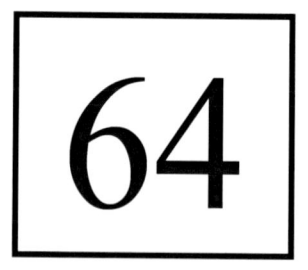

**As A Stock or Commodity
Thinketh In Its Heart So It Is**

$$\boxed{64}$$

IV : XII : XVI

"This book of the law shall not depart out of thy mouth; but thou shalt meditate therein day and night, that thou mayest observe to do according to all that is written therein: for then thou shalt make thy way prosperous, and then thou shalt have good success."

As A Stock or Commodity
Thinketh In Its Heart So It Is

Contents

Foreword viii

Chapter 1: Thought & The Character Of Commodities 1

Chapter 2: Effect of Thought on Circumstances & Business Environment.................................... 8

Chapter 3: Effect of Thought on The Health & The Body Of The Stock 30

Chapter 4: Thought & The Stock's Purpose 37

Chapter 5: The Commodity's Visions & Ideals 45

Chapter 6: Serenity 51

Appendix: Extracts From The Dictionary of Thoughts for Investors 57

Further Reading ix

Index xxii

**As A Stock or Commodity
Thinketh In Its Heart So It Is**

$$\boxed{43}$$

"For God requireth that which is past."

**As A Stock or Commodity
Thinketh In Its Heart So It Is**

Foreword

This book is based purely on The Art of Translation. In 1902 a gentleman by the name of James Allen published a book entitled As a Man Thinketh. This book was a "little volume (the result of meditation and experience) ... not intended as an exhaustive treatise on the much written upon subject of the power of thought". It went on to help (and continues to help) many people who's aim was (is) to understand the laws of thought and their effect on man's circumstances.

This too will be a short treatise with the main aim of setting firmly in the readers mind the whole basis of the Art of Foreknowledge in prices.

It is nothing new which is presented to the reader, although it may be a new way to understand the connection between thought and stocks and commodities. It is the scientifically minded reader who will benefit most from this perspective since through the firm understanding of the chapters in this book, shall he

As A Stock or Commodity
Thinketh In Its Heart So It Is

be able to understand the true basis and or cause of the economic events we experience.

It is suggestive rather than explanatory, its object being to stimulate men and women to the discovery and perception of the truth that -

"The stocks themselves are the makers of themselves"

by virtue of the thoughts which they absorb within their own fluctuations; that mind is the master weaver, both of the inner garment of character and the outer garment of business environment.

Many a time it is not prediction which is difficult, but understanding the natural basis of the laws that govern the future that are difficult to comprehend; and all it takes is a few men to aid the multitude in grasping that perspective which sets them off in the right direction.

**As A Stock or Commodity
Thinketh In Its Heart So It Is**

I encourage the reader to read this book over and over and over again until he may recite the main principles herein discussed -preferably with the eyes shut.

Nsingo Sakala.

13.02.12

**As A Stock or Commodity
Thinketh In Its Heart So It Is**

Chapter 1:
Thought & The Character Of Commodities

The aphorism, "As a Stock or commodity thinketh in its heart, so it is" not only embraces the whole of a commodity's being, but is so comprehensive as to reach out to every ordered and chaotic condition of a commodity's life. Prices are literally what men think, being governed by human energy; and their character reveals the complete sum of all the thoughts within a nation.

As the plant springs from, and could not be without, the seed, so every level of price, springs from the undetected pips of human thought, and could not have fluctuated or vibrated without them. This applies equally to those price levels believed to be "unexpected", "ground breaking" and "new" as to those which are premeditated through the primitive economic analyses of our day.

As A Stock or Commodity Thinketh In Its Heart So It Is

The motion of price is the flourishing of this human energy (or thought); and reveals the concealed 'heart beats' of the mind that governs all macro-economic amendments. The rises and declines of price levels are in themselves the fruits of their own making; thus does a commodity's own destiny lie in the sweet and bitter fruitage of its own husbandry.

The Art of Impulse suggests to us that "the impulses for any price level exist before the demand and supply for the goods themselves became manifest"; and that "we are usually only made aware of their prevalence long after their fruits have come forth." Moreover the Art of Yesterday reminds us that "a commodity's future is behind us" and that "since all men posses great hind-sight, we can all know it." What they are in number we manufactured and built. Thus does that adhesive concept of gamble or uncertainty become muted in the minds of the thinking man.

As A Stock or Commodity Thinketh In Its Heart So It Is

It matters little what the predominant consensus among economists is or what the political authorities decide to announce; and it matters little what the celebrities do or the majesty of a firm's new invention. Each commodity holds so persistently to its own breath and cycle that the rotations of these events, though seemingly substantial, are entirely different to those most commonly understood by the layman.

Thus in order to understand a commodity fully, you have to mentally attune your mind to its station in life – that is, to its vibration or frequency of activity in much the same manner that one tunes into Radio 1 on a Sunday morning, radio 2 on a Wednesday afternoon and Radio 3 on Friday evening. It has its own schedule and definition for "breaking news"; in the same manner that men have their own schedules for breaking news.

As A Stock or Commodity Thinketh In Its Heart So It Is

A commodity is a growth by law, and not a reaction to daily events, and cause and effect is as absolute and unwavering in its sphere of activities as in the world of visible and material things. The persistent application by the earnest individual, to the understanding of such laws, gifts that individual the Art of Foreknowledge. It is ironic however, that the expected levels of persistence are to be rigorously coupled with the mental capabilities of a child, as 'The Art of Childhood' so skilfully suggests.

Prices make and unmake themselves; and kitted with the armoury of human thought, they forge the weapons by which they annihilate themselves. They also fashion the tools with which they build for themselves heavenly mansions of prosperity; wealth and restfulness. By adopting the positive aspects of human thought, prices learn to ascend with the Divine Perfection of the Egyptian Gods. And it is a lofty learning process indeed – one that reveals prices' mastery in the Art of Knowledge.

As A Stock or Commodity
Thinketh In Its Heart So It Is

Furthermore by the adoption of the negative aspects of human energy, they descend with the distasteful qualities of a p- and a sh-. Between (and including) these two extremes are all the points of chemical personality that define the commodity.

Of all the beautiful truths pertaining to the power of human thought which have been restored and brought to light in this age by such works as The Secret, The Moses Code (and many other such works), none is more gladdening or fruitful of divine promise and confidence than this – that Price is the reflection of human thought, those moulders of current events; and silhouettes of economic conditions and monetary destiny.

"Only by much searching and mining are gold and diamonds obtained, and man can find every connection between this wonder we call 'thought' and 'reality' if he will dig deep into the mine of his own soul, using the language of prices as his

As A Stock or Commodity Thinketh In Its Heart So It Is

evidence of the things which he cannot see. The price of a man, for example is not external to himself. What a man gets paid for his services and consultations is the direct result of his predominant mental standing.

Moreover because humans are the architects of their own characters, and the builders of their destiny, they have the ability to visually and mathematically prove this if they so wish, without mystery; and without prejudice; and without superstition; if they but watch, control, and alter their thoughts and trace their effects upon mankind. This link (between cause and effect), they will find by patient practice and investigation (in the realm of prices) and by utilizing every experience, especially the most painful, as a means of obtaining that knowledge of themselves.

In this direction, as in no other, is the law absolute that 'He that seeketh (with The Art of Thaction) shall find; and to him that knocketh (with The Art of Beginning), it shall be opened"; for only by The Art of Persistence, The Art of Practice, and immutable Art of Silence can a man unerringly exclaim that: "As a Stock or commodity thinketh in its heart, so it is".

11

"What God hath given to a man,

God can taketh away"

**As A Stock or Commodity
Thinketh In Its Heart So It Is**

Chapter 2:
Effect of Thought on Circumstances & Business Environment

A commodity's mind may be likened to a garden, which may be intelligently cultivated or allowed to run wild; but whether cultivated or neglected, it must, and will, bring forth. If no useful seed patterns of thought are put into it, then an abundance of useless weed seeds will fall therein, and will continue to produce their kind.

Just as a gardener cultivates his plot, keeping it free from weeds, and growing the flowers and fruits which he requires, so may an investor tend to the garden of the stock and commodity markets, weeding out all the wrong, useless, and impure thought patterns, and cultivating toward perfection the flowers and fruits of right, useful, pure and permanent thought patterns. By pursuing this process, an investor sooner or later discovers that

As A Stock or Commodity
Thinketh In Its Heart So It Is

WITHIN the commodity itself is the master gardener or director of the price fluctuations he witnesses on the price chart. The investor is also well placed to reveal, from within the stock itself, the mathematical and alchemical laws of thought, and understands with ever-increasing accuracy, how the thought forces and mind elements operate in the shaping of, not only the commodity's character, circumstances, and destiny; but also the character circumstances and destiny of a nation.

Thought and character are one, and as character can only manifest and discover itself through environment and circumstance, the outer conditions of a commodity's life will always be found to be harmoniously related to its inner state. And since stocks are like electrons atoms or molecules, which hold persistently to their own individuality, it is possible for the scientifically inclined investor to fully understand and profit from this inner state. This does not mean that a

As A Stock or Commodity Thinketh In Its Heart So It Is

commodity's circumstances at any given time are an indication of its entire character, but that those circumstances are so intimately connected with some vital thought element within itself that, for the time being (until its master charts are identified), they are indispensable to its development.

Every stock is where it is by the law of its own being. The thoughts (which form the feminine aspect or the driving force of the stock) having been built into its character have brought it to its current price level, and in the arrangement of its life there is no element of chance, but all is the result of a law which cannot err. This is just as true of those stocks or commodities who are "out of harmony" with their fellow stocks and commodities on a particular exchange, as of those that move in harmony with them.

As A Stock or Commodity Thinketh In Its Heart So It Is

As a progressive and evolving entity, the commodity is where it is that it may, like man, learn that its life is a growth; and as it learns the spiritual lesson contained within its current fluctuations, the old fluctuations pass away and give place to other fluctuations.

Most traders in the markets believe that stocks are buffeted by circumstances and that they are mere creatures of Political, Economic, Social and Technological conditions. But when the wise investor realizes that he may place himself in a firm mental position so as to witness the hidden soil and seeds of this entity he calls 'a stock', he then becomes the scientific master of all the future occurrences concerning that entity.

That the economic environment grows out of thought every investor knows who has for any length of time spent enough time looking at his charts on the various timescales, for he will have

As A Stock or Commodity Thinketh In Its Heart So It Is

noticed that the alteration in the stock's fluctuations has been in exact proportion to an altered mental condition, which was initiated from within the stock itself, and NOT from without. So true is this that when an investor or trader earnestly applies himself to remedy the defects in his ability to read and understand the sacred language of the stock, by sitting and going over his charts alone in his office, he tends to make a swift and marked progression from mere analyst to scientific genius.

The stock, like nectar to a bee, attracts those investors who secretly harbour it; those who adore it, and also those whom are innately greedy and fear its sting. Not every investor, however, is able to profit from the stock, as it reaches the temperate heights of its cherished aspirations. Yes indeed the stock too has goals and dreams; and subsequently it falls to the level of its unchastened desires - and by understanding this entity from nature's perspective

As A Stock or Commodity Thinketh In Its Heart So It Is

is the means by which the investor is fully entitled to receive his profits.

Every thought seed sown or allowed to fall into the stock or commodity, and to take root there, produces its own, blossoming sooner or later into the acts of buying and selling made by the people trading it, and bearing its own fruitage in waves of prosperity and depression. Good thoughts bear prosperity, bad thoughts depression.

The economic environment shapes itself to the inner world of thought, and both pleasant and unpleasant external conditions are factors which make for the ultimate good of the individual stock. As the reaper of its own harvest, the stock therefore learns both by suffering and bliss. That is, by having both downtrends and uptrends.

A commodity, therefore, does not come to its position by the tyranny of fate of circumstance, but

As A Stock or Commodity Thinketh In Its Heart So It Is

by the pathway of grovelling thoughts and base desires of the people thinking about it, whether consciously or subconsciously. Nor does a well seasoned stock fall suddenly into decline by stress of any mere external force; the negative phase in its fluctuations had long been secretly fostered in the stock's heart, and the actual declining phase was simply the appointed hour of when its downward trend was to be revealed.

By Nature's Law, external influences do not make the stock act the way it does; and it is the stock itself, which reveals this to investor. No such conditions can exist as "the stock is declining because of today's rumours" and/or similar so called "key influences". And the investor, therefore, as a scientific practitioner, is in a position to understand the cause, the shaper and author of the stock's motion. Even at birth the stock comes into its own, and through every step of its ethereal pilgrimage it attracts those combinations of elements which reveal its being, which are the reflections of its own purity and impurity, its strength and weakness, its actions and reactions.

Thus stocks do not behave in accordance with any other law but their own, and tend to remain that which they are in the majority of cases. On the chart is where their whims, fancies, and ambitions are recorded at every step; and their inmost fluctuations (that is, their causes) both positive and negative, are fed with their own food. It is perhaps the case that the traded stocks and commodities scream from the mount of the exchanges that: "O investor, why sulkest thou? The divinity that shapes our ends is in ourselves; it is our very self, as you yourself are your very own. Our fates are imprisoned by your thoughts yet you do not see that it is indeed so, in both time and price."

Not what the investor wishes and prays for does the stock become, but what it openly tells the investor it will become. The investor's wishes and prayers are

As A Stock or Commodity Thinketh In Its Heart So It Is

only gratified and answered when they harmonize with the vibration of the thoughts and actions that govern market movements.

In the light of this truth, what, then, is the meaning of "no one can predict the stock market"? It means that men have been continually revolting against the external effects of a stock, while all the time they are nourishing and preserving their ignorance of its cause in their hearts. For the cause of stock patterns is the same as the cause of man's patterns. That cause is subtle but never stubborn. Ignoring it serves to retard the efforts of the trader in making consistent profits, and thus keeps his uncertainty about the course of future prices needing remedy.

Men are so anxious to make a fortune in the financial markets, but are unwilling to gain the relevant knowledge required to get them there. They therefore remain scalpers in the market, scrambling for a few points at a time, when the

As A Stock or Commodity
Thinketh In Its Heart So It Is

huge profits are in the long pull swings. The investor who does not shrink from this self-crucifixion and studies those things which market enthusiasts usually abhor can never fail to accomplish the object upon which his heart is set. The future will become an open book and the investor's greatest fears will be no more. This is as true of earthly things as of heavenly things.

Here is a man who is wretchedly poor. He is extremely anxious that he can make quick profits in the market in order to improve his surroundings and home comforts. Yet all the time he shirks the work required in order that he may LEARN before he loses, and considers he is justified in trying to gamble his way to financial freedom on the grounds of the insufficiency of time and money. Such a man does not understand the simplest rudiments of those principles which are the basis of true success in trading. He is not only totally unfitted to rise out of his wretchedness, but is actually attracting to

As A Stock or Commodity
Thinketh In Its Heart So It Is

himself a still deeper wretchedness by dwelling in, and acting out, indolent, deceptive, and undisciplined thoughts. The same wretchedness befalls any man, even the rich, so long as they invest on hope alone.

I have introduced this case merely as illustration of the truth that behind the stock itself is the cause (though nearly always never detected) of its fluctuations and the investor requires nothing more than its past record of transactions. That, while the investor may be aiming to get good profits, he is continually frustrating its accomplishment by disregarding the mathematical basis of thoughts and desires (and their relations to prices) which cannot possibly harmonize with that end. Such cases could be multiplied and varied almost indefinitely, but this is not necessary. The reader can, if he so resolves, trace the action of the laws of thought in a chosen commodity from any exchange by watching and learning its habits from time to time, and until

As A Stock or Commodity
Thinketh In Its Heart So It Is

this is done, mere external facts cannot serve as a ground of reasoning for investing in anything.

Circumstances, however, are so complicated, thought is so deeply rooted, and the waves vary so vastly amongst the individual stocks and commodities, that a stock's entire life structure and permanent charts cannot always be judged by another from the external aspect of its patterns alone. The internal mechanics of the thing may have to be entered into so as to shed light on the scientific basis of the motion being analysed.

It is common knowledge that an investor may quite genuinely have the desire to be able to pick the direction in the trend of stocks, yet suffer losses. Another may not be so interested in the long term trend and trade 'on impulse', yet acquire wealth from his operations. The one man fails because his mind is inharmoniously connected to the stocks which he attempts to profit from, leading to the

As A Stock or Commodity Thinketh In Its Heart So It Is

losses he endures. The other succeeds because, whether he realised it consciously or not he makes his operations according to natural law. In the light of a deeper knowledge of self and wider experience, such judgment is found to be correct.

It is pleasing to human vanity to believe that man is above nature. But not until a man has tried his hand at trading a stock for profit without rules does he eventually erase this sickly, bitter, and impure thought from his mind. It is only when the investor decides to appreciate nature's language in the markets when he can be in a position to know and declare that his prior losses were the result of his lack of knowledge of the causal component instead of any external factor like the news. And on the way to that supreme knowledge, he will have found working in his mind and life, the Great Law which is absolutely just, and which cannot err to reward the investor who has worked hard and earned his ability to forecast the future correctly. Possessed of

As A Stock or Commodity
Thinketh In Its Heart So It Is

such knowledge, he will then know, looking back upon his past ignorance and blindness, that the seemingly muffled fluctuations in all stocks are, and always were, justly ordered, and that all their past experiences, both the good uptrends and seemingly bad downtrends, were the equitable outworking of each stock's evolving self.

Good thought patterns can never produce bad trends in the future. Bad thought patterns can never produce good trends in the future. This is but saying that nothing can come from corn but corn, nothing from nettles but nettles. Investors understand this law in the natural world, and work with it. But few understand it in the financial world (though its operation there is just as simple and undeviating), and they, therefore, end up with losses.

The difficulty experienced in forecasting the trend of commodities is always the effect of using the

As A Stock or Commodity Thinketh In Its Heart So It Is

wrong approach in tackling the problem. It is an indication that the individual is out of harmony with himself and with the fundamental Law of all existence. The sole and supreme use of losses actually is to force the investor to purify and to burn out all that is useless and impure in his operations. Losses are greatly minimized and profits greatly increased for the investor who is pure in thought.

The stock also has to, by law, go through periods of pain and suffering. The circumstances in which a stock encounters 'suffering' (or great declines) are the result of mental enharmony manifesting within the stock itself. The circumstances which a stock encounters with blessedness (that is during its period of a rising trend) is the measure of right thought, and is rightly measured using right angled triangles and the letters of the alphabet. Wretchedness (that is during its period of a falling trend), is the measure of wrong thought and is also

As A Stock or Commodity Thinketh In Its Heart So It Is

measured geometrically using the letters of the alphabet. A stock may, at one and the same time decline when good news comes out; and may rise when bad news comes out. Rising trends and good news are only joined together when the news cycle vibrates at the same keynote as the stock cycle - something which only the wise investor can calculate from the mind. And a declining stock only descends at the same time as bad news when the negative vibrations in the two cycles are one and the same, at the same time.

An investor only begins to be wise when he ceases to whine and revile and blame external factors for his losses, and commences to search for the hidden justice which regulates the motion of prices (that which I have termed the divine motion). And as he adapts his mind to that regulating factor, he ceases to accuse others as the cause of his misjudging of the trend, and builds himself up in a strong and noble base of knowledge for his trading business.

As A Stock or Commodity Thinketh In Its Heart So It Is

He ceases to kick against circumstances, but begins to use them as aids to his more rapid progress, and as a means of discovering the hidden powers and possibilities within himself, and within stocks and commodities.

Law, not chaos, is the dominating principle in the markets as it is in the universe. Justice, not injustice, is the soul and substance of each stock's life. And righteousness, not corruption, is the moulding and moving force in the spiritual government of the financial markets. This being so, the investor has but to right himself to find that the stock market is already perfect and right in its imperfection; and during the process of putting himself right, he will find that as he alters his thoughts toward scientific lines, as opposed to financial lines, the whole meaning and purpose of science will in fact alter toward him.

As A Stock or Commodity
Thinketh In Its Heart So It Is

The proof of this truth is in every single stock. In fact more so in the commodities for they are products derived directly from nature's womb, and they therefore admit of easy investigation by systematic introspection and scientific analysis. Let an investor radically alter his thoughts, and he will be astonished at the rapid transformation it will effect in his ability to read the future, and most importantly - himself.

Some investors and manipulators who have already grasped the laws and apply it, imagine that thought can be kept secret, but it cannot. It is on the tape every market day of the year. Freely available for those who are bold enough to stare it in the face. It rapidly crystallizes into habitual price swings in each stock, and the habit solidifies into habits of prosperity and depression, which solidify into circumstances of love and war. In fact wheat prices forecast future wars and impure thoughts of every kind crystallize into clearly measurable geometric

As A Stock or Commodity Thinketh In Its Heart So It Is

entities which only the initiated can apprehend, thus debunking the exaggerated effects of adverse external circumstances. Thoughts of fear, thoughts of buying, thoughts of selling, thoughts of success and thoughts of coming pain ALL show forth on the chart before the reality hits. Hence why the wise become no longer slavishly dependent on 'current' events when confidently determining future trends.

A particular train of thought persisted in by the stock, be it good or bad, cannot fail to produce its results on the character and future prospects of a commodity. This 'train' can be mechanically manufactured by the man who understands the working of the stock's time or its "wheels within wheels" as Ezekiel says. It is perhaps true that the stock itself cannot directly choose the environment in which it is traded, but it can establish and does establish the boundaries within which the price can and will move according to its date of birth, name and numbers; and so indirectly, yet surely, shape its own circumstances.

Nature helps every stock and commodity to the gratification of the thought patterns which it most encourages, and opportunities are presented to the intuitive investor who can play along with nature's game, which we call life.

Let the wise man learn in silence and subjection and cease from his awful habit of settling for economic opinions that have no arithmetical basis; and all the world, yay all the stocks and commodities, will soften toward him, and be ready to help him attain his wealth. Let him put away his weakly and sickly thoughts, and lo! opportunities to learn more about the world will spring up on every stock he analyses to aid him in creating a better world. Let him become an adept at identifying the lasting thoughts within any market he comes across, and no hard fate shall bind him down to

As A Stock or Commodity
Thinketh In Its Heart So It Is

wretchedness and shame. The stock's own thinking is his kaleidoscope, and the varying combinations of colours which it presents to him are the exquisitely adjusted pictures of its ever moving thoughts. A picture is worth a thousand words. Yay even more - a billion dollars!

> It will be what it wills to be;
> Let busy bodies find its false content
> In that poor word, "environment,"
> But Nature's Law scorns it, and sets it free.

> It masters time and conquers space;
> It cows that boastful trickster, Chance,
> And bids the tyrant Circumstance

> The Universal Will, that force unseen,
> The offspring of a deathless Soul,
> Shows the stock the way to its goal,
> Though walls of periodicity intervene.

**As A Stock or Commodity
Thinketh In Its Heart So It Is**

Be not impatient in delay,

But wait as one who understands;

For when knowledge is grasped, it multiplies,

And the God within you will expand.

10

*"For a good tree bringeth not forth corrupt fruit; neither doth
a corrupt tree bring forth good fruit."*

Chapter 3:
Effect of Thought on Health & The Body Of The Stock

The price of a commodity is a servant to the universal mind. It obeys the operations of thoughts, whether they be deliberately chosen by manipulators in the market or automatically expressed. At the bidding of unlawful thoughts the price sinks rapidly into disease and decay; at the command of glad and beautiful thoughts it rises, becoming clothed with youthfulness and beauty. This can be positively proven when one looks at the price charts.

Thus disease and health, which are commonly referred to as busts and booms, are rooted in thought. Sickly thoughts will express themselves through sickly price activity. Thoughts of worry and fear about economic conditions have been known to lead to declines in price. The stocks, for example,

As A Stock or Commodity Thinketh In Its Heart So It Is

whose investors live in fear of loss are the stocks which end up declining and lead those same investors to the loss which they feared. Anxiety quickly demoralizes the whole body of the entity, and lays it open to the entrance of disease; while impure thoughts, even if not physically indulged in, will soon shatter its nervous system. The investor is here reminded that each stock's physical representation is analogous to the human body, and the analogy is proven to be correct based on biological and mathematical calculations.

Strong, pure, and happy thoughts build up the stock's body in vigour and grace. The body is a delicate and plastic instrument, which responds readily to investors' thoughts by which it is impressed, and habits of thought will produce the patterns you see on the chart, be they considered good or bad.

As A Stock or Commodity
Thinketh In Its Heart So It Is

Stocks will continue to have periods of decline so long as the investors themselves propagate impure, unclean thoughts. Out of a clean heart (consider the mathematical cardioid whenever you see the word 'heart') comes a clean life and a clean body. Out of a defiled mind proceeds a defiled life and corrupt body. Thought is the fountain of action, life and manifestation; and because the fountain of thought for stocks is pure, the future price action tends to be pure, which garners its predictability.

The market can be considered to have what I would call a perfect body, and this is only possible because it is guarded (as well as guided) by the universal mind, the cause of all its movements.

Each time this body is renewed, the "beautiful" manifests on the price chart. A sight that those with a holy imagination appreciate and understand as being not only miraculous - but also wonderfully bound by God's immutable laws.

As A Stock or Commodity
Thinketh In Its Heart So It Is

I have analyzed many stocks of various ages and it is apparent that they do possess the same characteristics as human beings. There is one particular one, whose body I sketched out recently, which was born in the 1970s and yet has the bright, innocent face of a child. I know of another, whose birth day came in June 2003, whose face is drawn into inharmonious contours. The one, the investor may say, is the result of a sweet and sunny disposition; the other is the outcome of lack of passion and discontent. In astrology they use the terms 'good aspects' and 'bad aspects' for the former and the latter respectively.

As man himself cannot have a sweet and wholesome abode unless he admits the air and sunshine freely into his soul, so does a strong body and a bright, happy, or serene countenance for the stock only result from the free admittance into its mind of thoughts of joy and good will and serenity.

As A Stock or Commodity Thinketh In Its Heart So It Is

We find this idea well documented in astrological texts, though the wording may perhaps be slightly misleading. Certain sectors in the heavens have the elements of air, water, earth and fire; those which are analogous to the same elements required in agricultural pursuits here on earth. - And this is an important law to remember.

On the faces of the majority of aged stocks (referred to as seasoned stocks in other texts) there are wrinkles made by sympathy, others by strong and pure thought, others are carved by passion. At the writing of this text many cannot distinguish them in a stock, though they can most certainly distinguish them in men. With those who have lived righteously, age is calm, peaceful, and softly mellowed, like the setting sun. There was recently a banking stock which was summoned to its deathbed. It was not old in man's definition of years, but on the chart it had in fact gone though the entire life sequence that all entities go through

As A Stock or Commodity Thinketh In Its Heart So It Is

albeit in a short space of time. As a result its purpose was achieved and it died as violently (that is with many rapid fluctuations) as it had lived, though it was a sweet and peaceful death when viewed from nature's perspective.

There is no perspective like nature's perspective for witnessing the mood of a stock. And there is no better acquired mind than God's mind for understanding and translating this mood into practical applications, thus dispersing the shadows of uncertainty and doubt in scientific pursuits.

For the investor to live continually in thoughts of suspicion, and scepticism of God's presence in the markets and the investor's ability to understand it, is to be confined in a self-made prison hole. But to think well of all, to be open minded and persistent enough to patiently learn to prove the cause in all fluctuations - is to open the portals of heaven and

**As A Stock or Commodity
Thinketh In Its Heart So It Is**

to dwell day to day in the company of the greatest men and women the world hath ever known.

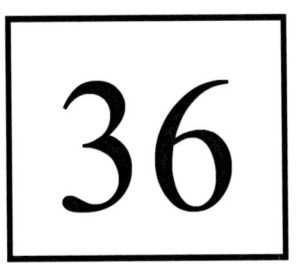

36

"It was planted in a good soil by great waters, that it might bring forth branches, and that it might bear fruit, that it might be a goodly vine."

**As A Stock or Commodity
Thinketh In Its Heart So It Is**

Chapter 4:
Thought & The Stock's Purpose

Until thought is linked scientifically with time and price there is no intelligent accomplishment in the field of investment. No matter how advanced our technology becomes or how complex our thinking seems to evolve, there will be no real progress made by any investor until he or she realizes that the stock already has within it the key algorithm that foretells its own future. It is because of this inbuilt 'code' that the thinking man is able to make accurate forecasts without spending days, weeks or months in front of a computer, "programming".

The program has already been written - all we have to do is learn how to read it. The rest of the time is to be spent in appreciation of the entity that devised it.

As A Stock or Commodity Thinketh In Its Heart So It Is

With the majority or traders the bark of thought is allowed to "drift" to the back of their analyses like it is some annoying virus to be avoided. Aimlessness is a vice, and such drifting must not continue for him who would steer clear of chaos and uncertainty.

It is evident that if stocks did not have a central purpose in themselves they would easily fall prey to investors worries, fears, troubles, and self-pityings, all of which would be indications of indecision and confusion on the part of the mind that guides the stock. This would be akin to sin (though by a different perspective) on the universal mind's part, since confusion and indecision leads to failure, unhappiness, and chaotic outcomes. Fortunately this is not the case as most traders are well aware. Stocks vibrate at all times, according to their established purpose, which is usually re-iterated at the beginning of every major move either up or down. This is why I consider their motion as 'holy' - because they never err in their feat. Though I myself, being human, may still err in my translations of the message it conveys.

Thus as a righteous man conceives a legitimate purpose in his heart, and sets out to accomplish it, so does a stock or commodity conceive its purpose BEFORE it sets out to accomplish it. This purpose is the centralizing point of its motion. It may take the form of a spiritual ideal in much the same way that man has spiritual ideals, according to the time and season.

I look forward to the day when all investors can witness this phenomenon with their own eyes. When they can see the stock steadily focus thought forces upon the object which it has set before it. For it ignites an inspiration that no man can set alight. The investor should therefore make witnessing this 'purpose' his supreme duty, and should devote himself to its comprehension, not allowing his thoughts to wander away into ephemeral fancies, longings, and imaginings. This is the royal road to knowledge and true concentration of thought.

No doubt he will fail again and again to see the true power of the words here laid down (as he necessarily must until weakness of mind is overcome). However, the strength of character gained will be the measure of his true success, and this will form a new starting point for future wealth, power and triumph.

Those who are not prepared for the apprehension of nature's laws as applicable to the financial markets, will (simply put) - "not get it" until they prepare themselves by seeking the kingdom of God, which is within them, as the Bible clearly states. All this may seem insignificant and unconnected to the accumulation of wealth but if the investor would fix his thoughts upon this task diligently and without ceasing, he will find resolution and develop enough energy, for him to connect the subtle dots that reveal the full picture behind my words.

"In the beginning was the word, and the word was with God, and the word was God."

Even the stock in the weakest position, knowing its own weakness, and knowing that strength can only be developed by effort and practice, will at once begin to exert itself in the upward direction, and adding effort to effort, patience to patience, and strength to strength, will never cease to develop, and will at last grow divinely strong, turning its downtrend into a feverishly powerful uptrend.

As the physically weak man is made strong by careful and patient training, so the stock of weak thoughts is made strong only by being impressed by an accumulation of right thinking among traders.

As A Stock or Commodity Thinketh In Its Heart So It Is

Having conceived of its purpose, a stock mentally marks out a straight pathway to its achievement, looking neither to the right nor to the left. "Straightness" to the stock, it must be remembered, is not the same concept of linearity that man is taught to grasp in his early life.

Doubts and fears about this should be rigorously excluded; they are disintegrating elements which hinder the investor from exclaiming: "yay I have witnessed it ... And it is indeed so". This straight line of effort for the commodity, is rendered crooked, ineffectual and useless in man's mind. Which is incorrect from nature's perspective. Consider the river, any river, whether on earth or in the heavens. Do any of them exhibit the "straightness", which man commonly refers to as "straight"? Or do they all in fact tell crooked tales, which from their own perspective, render them straight and perfect in every way.

As A Stock or Commodity Thinketh In Its Heart So It Is

The stock's purpose, energy and power to do, all cease to be 'visible' when the investor's doubt and fear creep in. Lo! Prove all things and hold fast to that which is good.

The will to do springs from the knowledge that we can do. Doubt and fear are the great enemies of knowledge, and he who encourages them, who does not slay them, thwarts himself at every step.

He who has conquered doubt and fear has conquered failure. His every thought is allied with power, and all difficulties are bravely met and wisely overcome. The stock and/or commodity's purposes are seasonably planted, and they bloom and bring forth fruit which does not fall prematurely to the ground.

Spend time watching this phenomenon in order to understand why "Thought allied fearlessly to purpose becomes creative force."

**As A Stock or Commodity
Thinketh In Its Heart So It Is**

He who knows this is ready to become something higher and stronger than a trader or investor analyzing the fluctuating sensations of the masses (as reflected in price). He who does this has become the conscious and intelligent scientist and inventor.

...

24

"Either make the tree good, and his fruit good; or else make the tree corrupt, and his fruit corrupt: for the tree is known by his fruit"

Chapter 5:
The Commodity's Visions & Ideals

The dreamers have the most potential to understand the cause behind market movements. As what is visible to the eye is sustained by the invisible, so the fluctuation of stocks, through time, pattern and price, are nourished by the beautiful visions of their solitary dreams. Humanity cannot forget the power of dreams, and commodities are the most tangible tools we have to remind us of their importance. For it is through their laws we are reminded that we all live in dreams; and that persistence and understanding will some day reveal to us the mathematical realities which we shall one day see and know.

Composer, sculptor, painter, poet, prophet, sage, geographer, astronomy and inventor - these are the makers of the afterworld, the architects of heaven.

As A Stock or Commodity Thinketh In Its Heart So It Is

And to the scientific investor is the mastery of all these professions perhaps most likely to be gifted, since knowledge of stocks is the knowledge of thoughts. And the knowledge of thoughts is the knowledge of all.

It is because the stock cherishes a beautiful vision, a lofty ideal in its own heart, that it will one day realize it. And past records prove this assertion. Through the understanding of prices we may more confidently dream to discover a new world, and we will discover it. We may foster the vision of a multiplicity of worlds and a wider universe, and within a short period we will reveal it. We may behold the vision of heaven and a spiritual world of stainless beauty and perfect peace, and we will enter into it.

Cherish the visions the stock reveals to you. Cherish its ideals. Cherish the music that stirs in its heart, the beauty that forms in its mind, the

As A Stock or Commodity Thinketh In Its Heart So It Is

loveliness that drapes its purest thoughts, for out of them will grow all the stock's future price movements, all future news and business environments; because the stock WILL remain true to them, and its world will at last be built directly from them.

To desire is to obtain; to aspire is to achieve. Desire and aspiration manifests as the elements of "time, price and pattern" in the stock, and all three are necessary to measure the extent to which the stock will "obtain and achieve" its future trends. Such are the lessons given to man by the ancients, that is: "what ye desire ye should ask and ye shall receive it." Whosoever has questioned whether this works, need only witness its manifestation in the markets.

As the learned investor, you will know you have mastered the craft to the fullest extent when you can confidently prove that the stock's "Vision" is the

As A Stock or Commodity Thinketh In Its Heart So It Is

promise of what it shall one day be. Its Ideal is the prophecy of what it shall at last unveil.

The greatest rise a stock or commodity has experienced in the past was at first and for a time a dream. Its oak slept soundly in its acorn; its bird waited in the egg; and in the highest vision of its own soul a waking angel stirred. Its Dreams were clearly the seedlings of its realities. There is no mystery or occultness in these things. The future is at all times behind the investor, and all he has to do is find it.

Thus in all stocks and commodities, as in human affairs, there are efforts, and there are results, and the strength of the effort is the measure of the result. Chance is not. Uptrends, declines, sideways movements, expectations and surprise news are the fruits of effort. They are to the stock as thoughts completed, dreams accomplished and visions realized.

As A Stock or Commodity Thinketh In Its Heart So It Is

The vision that stocks keep in their minds, the Ideal that they enthrone in their heart - this is what they will build their life by, this is what they will become.

Many will scoff and laugh at these words, yet the proof is in the mathematical accuracy of the forecasts that the investor will be able to create once he fully internalizes what has been mentioned. It is about time that men of science also take notice of the 'law of thought' as it works within price. For through it many scientific breakthroughs in many industries may be accomplished with only a fraction of the time and a fraction of the money.

In order to "Prove all things and hold fast to that which is good", it is recommended that the investor stick to one class of stocks; study them day and night; never diverting his attention to other lines until he grasps the mathematical method which enables him to forecast stocks many months and

**As A Stock or Commodity
Thinketh In Its Heart So It Is**

years in advance. He will then realize that the law that governs the motion of thought is no different to the law of harmonic analysis as utilized in music, physics, electricity, radio and Blueprint squares.

13

*"Prophet Yunus was in a whale's mouth for 40 days...
And Jonah began to enter into the city a day's journey,
and he cried, and said, Yet forty days, and Nineveh shall
be overthrown."*

**As A Stock or Commodity
Thinketh In Its Heart So It Is**

Chapter 6:
Serenity

Calmness of mind is one of the beautiful jewels embodied within the wisdom of a stock. It is the result of long and patient effort in The Art of Gravity or Self-Control. Its presence is an indication of the ripening of a stock, whose fluctuations are in themselves produced from the calm waters of Nun. By knowing the location of these waters the investor can hope to enjoy a more than ordinary knowledge of the laws and operations of thought. Thus being rendered the power to PROVE those many things which have been written about thought substance in recent years.

The investor himself becomes calm in the measure that he understands himself as a thought-evolved being, for such knowledge necessitates the understanding of price movement as the result of

As A Stock or Commodity Thinketh In Its Heart So It Is

thought - the causal substance. As he develops a right understanding, and sees more and more clearly the internal relations of things by the action of cause and effect, he ceases to fuss and fume and worry and grieve, and remains poised, steadfast and serene. He does indeed "gain nerve" from his knowledge, and becomes independent of the petty fears which grip the un-wise investors.

The calm man, having learned how to govern himself first, before embarking on his monetary business, knows how to adapt himself to changing economic conditions; and hence get out of his positions at the right time. - A feat which many market enthusiasts and commentators have often deemed impossible. Upon SEEING the abilities of the investor who uses Natural Laws, they will in time have nothing left but reverence for his investing 'gifts', and feel that they can learn from him and rely upon him to ascertain the future of prices.

As A Stock or Commodity Thinketh In Its Heart So It Is

It is often said that 'the more tranquil the investor becomes, the greater is his success, his influence, his power for good'. In the world of the price-lander (that is the stock or commodity) the same laws apply. As it was in the beginning of our world, when 'the Earth was void and darkness was upon the face of the deep'; so it is in the world of the stock. - From this moment (if i may be allowed to call it such) comes forth the most powerful details outlining the commodity's entire existence. Even the ordinary relatively unpopular stock, with low volume of transactions, will find this law to be a firm part of its DNA. It is the existence of this period of tranquillity which 'locks in' the powerful force of gravity (or self-control); and equanimity, within those stocks that people tend to love and trade in.

The calm investor is always loved and revered. He is like a shade-giving tree in a thirsty land, or a

As A Stock or Commodity Thinketh In Its Heart So It Is

sheltering rock in a storm; and he is always aware of his duty to gifting others his confidence should they desire it. I affirm that ALL commodities move with tranquil hearts, despite their seemingly violent fluctuations. They are sweet-tempered and balanced, most especially so when they are at the beginning of their cycles. It will not matter to the natural investor, whether it rains or shines, or what changes are said to affect the motion of a stock's price because he comes to KNOW the sweet blessings possessed by the commodity and is assured, well in advance that the commodity itself will be made always sweet, serene, and calm.

That exquisite poise of character which we call serenity is the most powerful lesson in investing, and most fittingly the last. When a man has nerve, he will be able to use his knowledge in the flowering of his wealth, by taking advantage of the fruitage of the stock. It is as precious as wisdom, more to be desired than gold - yea, than even fine gold!! How insignificant and confused mere money-seekers look in comparison with the serene, understanding investor - The type that dwells in the ocean of Truth, beneath the waves of THE DEEP, beyond the reach of tempest waters; and in the Eternal waters of Wealth and Calm!

"How many investors do we know who sour their lives, who ruin all that is sweet and beautiful through trading commodities, who destroy their poise of character, become greedy and sometimes mentally insane!?! If they only but understood that the stocks which they trade already bears the brunt of their gravity, then they would not ruin their lives and mar their happiness by lack of knowledge and self-control. How few people we meet in life who are well-balanced, who have that exquisite poise which is characteristic of the finished character!"

Yes, the investment profession surges with uncontrolled greed, is tumultuous with ungoverned grief, is blown about by anxiety, doubt and confusion. Yet God has given us the power to lay these heavy burdens on the stock. Only the wise man, only he whose thoughts are controlled and purified, makes the winds and the storms of price obey him.

Tempest-tossed souls, wherever ye may be, under whatsoever conditions ye may live, know this - in the ocean of life the isles of Blessedness are smiling, and sunny shore of your ideal awaits your coming. Keep your hand firmly upon the helm of the commodity's thought patterns. In the bark of its soul reclines the commanding Master; He never sleeps as he is forever commanding the commodity's ship. The investor's self-control will present him with strength and his right thought with reveal his hidden ability to know the future of prices and profit by it.

"For God giveth to a man that is good in his sight, wisdom, and knowledge, and joy."

**As A Stock or Commodity
Thinketh In Its Heart So It Is**

Appendix:
Extracts From The Dictionary of Thoughts for Investors

The following 'thoughts' were taken from the "Dictionary of Thoughts" (D.O.T.s) by Nsingo Sakala and may prove valuable to the reader of this work.

...

Change: Change is the law of life for man, but not for price. If man was to accept his Godly nature, neither would he need to change. For he would already BE all the changes possible.

Childhood: Like humans, all commodities, in childhood are the most celebrated of artists; They, however, have less difficulty remaining artists once grown up.

Courage: Any man or woman can make opinions on the destination of prices. He or she can make them seem more busy; and more complex than they actually are. It takes a creative genius with heaps of courage to move in the reverse, more scientific direction.

Decay: Decay is inherent in all compounded things. This is most evident in the declining phase of price motion. This phase is also born in the cradle with growth.

Disclosure: All events, whether past, present or future, are openly revealed. To disclose events in advance of their occurrence would be beneficial only to those willing to understand* the cause.

As A Stock or Commodity Thinketh In Its Heart So It Is

Doing: Prices determine never to be idle. Infinite is the number of price levels that can be reached by them, because they are always 'doing'."

Dreams: Prices go confidently in the direction of their dreams. This is how they manage to live the life they imagined.

Fear: The fear of applying foreign principles to prices is the main source of superstition in the field, and one of the main sources of financial loss. To conquer this fear is the beginning of wisdom.

Fiction: Fiction allures to the knotty task of figuring price movements by enlightening the imagination and striking out the ego. The inflated fantasies of the Gods reveal the illuminated reality of this motion.

Fulfilment: Every fluctuation that prices perform, whether up or down, will lead them to the destination where their causative thoughts intend them to go. There is no direction which is right or wrong, except that which is against the rhythm of the commodity's song. When the song ends, the fulfilment is achieved; but just before then, the song begins again.

How: There are those who have already figured most of what is written in these pages and can apply them accordingly to the accumulation of their wealth. They simply did what you they were supposed to do.

Humanity: The language of Humanity is firmly engraved on the price chart. Prices move in relation to some

As A Stock or Commodity Thinketh In Its Heart So It Is

fundamental vibration or keynote, which determines the unity in their chords of expression or fluctuation.

Humility: In order to discover the entire knowledge hidden within price, one has to be humble in its presence, without prejudice and without greed.

Illusion: The ordinary economics, or pure economics, cannot be an object of the arts. Illusory economics on the grounds of faith is the secret of the fine Art of foreknowledge in prices.

Impulse: A price impulse is a point of departure or exodus. As soon as it establishes itself, it becomes fuelled by thought.

Insanity: He, who believes that nature's laws govern the motion of prices without feeling somewhat insane in the face of men, quickly loses favour with the Gods.

Judgment: People often abhor studying nature's laws in order to profit by them because they do not know them; and they will not know them because they abhor studying.

Learning: One can learn much about oneself and the world at large through the understanding of Price motion. He may obtain from this tool, a method by which he may learn all that there is to know about TIME, SPACE but most importantly – GOD.

Life: Prices, like life are the effects of resolute thoughts going forth. They motion through in cyclic chord, strictly according to nature's law.

Mass: As the mass of a commodity increases so

As A Stock or Commodity Thinketh In Its Heart So It Is

does the characteristics of its motion periodically recur. Not capriciously but at regular intervals.

Motion: All motion is curved and all motion is exponentially bound. Prices though linear they may seem, are also bound in the curves of motion with the rest of life.

Mystery: It is enough if one tries merely to comprehend a little of the mysteries of price every day. The more time spent in study, the less of a mystery is soon becomes.

Number: The properties of prices are the properties of the essentials, which are the properties of numbers.

Opportunity: The opportunities to make money through the understanding of price motion are literally infinite since the law in the price of one commodity is the exact same law in all other commodities.

Passion: Zeal is the fire of the astute investor. Its consistent application will lead even the least educated of men to monetary gain.

Perspective: If from man's point of view, the ability to prophecy on prices is impossible, but from God's point of view it is impossible. Then why is it that men choose to remain men?

Plagiarism: Since man is in the fortunate position to be able to comprehend the workings of nature, he should not be afraid to copy that which he learns from her; especially that which helps him benefit from the cycles in price movements.

As A Stock or Commodity Thinketh In Its Heart So It Is

Poverty: All commodities like to live as poor men with lots of money.

Practice: The maxim practice makes purpose is most easily evidenced when one witnesses the number of times prices attempt to 'reach their destinies' within a particular period. It is usually after the third attempt, when their 'lives' become what which they had been practicing.

Preparation: It is, indeed, the duty of a knowing man to warn the people of what is coming so that they may prepare for prosperity or trouble ahead.

Property: The greatest value that a man can attain from investment activities is that of being able to own, copy and distribute the creations which he has been responsible for.

Push: Prices just keep pushing. They just keep pushing. They make every mistake that could be made. But in the end, they get to their destination; simply because they just keep pushing.

Questions: Important questions will always arise in the investor's mind. Questions like "what do I buy" and "what do I sell" "where do I buy and where do I sell", "whose council should I seek and whose council should I avoid. Valid as they all are, the answers to these questions lack in importance compared to those answers derived from the question: "WHEN do I buy and WHEN do I sell."

Reading: If you listen carefully, you may be able to hear the ticker scream, albeit very silently: "I beg

As A Stock or Commodity Thinketh In Its Heart So It Is

you read me from my perspective, not yours!"

Reflection: A commodity travels more usefully, than a man, because each one, having grown up alone, reflects more.

Repetition: Price motions repeat themselves, and work according to past cycles. These cycles are there for us to understand when we but pay them our divine attention. Repetition is necessary so that all men, from all generations have an equal chance to learn the order inherent within the universe.

Sex: In all of nature, it is through sexual activity that conception takes place. As humans conceive, prices will also conceive.

Signs: The patterns on the price chart are the signatures of a divine mind. By learning the signs and figuring their mathematics, you will be able to know in advance how to succeed according to these signs and hence the season.

Silence: Every great teacher on the practical application of natural principles to price is dead, except silence.

Sound: A commodity's price like crystals, will oscillate at a frequency according to its diameter and elements.

The City: Let us imagine the hydrological cycle for a moment. Water evaporates, it condenses and then it precipitates. It evaporates, it condenses and then it precipitates. It evaporates, it condenses and then it precipitates. Apply this faithfully to your analyses.

As A Stock or Commodity
Thinketh In Its Heart So It Is

Thought: Thoughts are not afraid to die; therefore, there is nothing they cannot achieve. Every fuelled impulse of thought or idea has courage enough to inspire a nation. The levels of inspiration, in our time, can be measured in price.

Time: By working towards thinking of prices cyclically one will be greatly aided in viewing the world as one whole.

Valence: So government bonds, corporate bonds, greedy bonds, devilish bonds and angelic bonds - they all abide by nature's bond.

Wealth: Now if you think that you can amass great wealth using these principles without* having to share it or help others grasp it, think again.

When: Any man of sound of business does best when he keeps up to date with the pricing seasons for his goods. Now this expression ""up-to-date"" should not be kept so empty (or vague) as men currently see it.

Who: Be the "who" that quits wasting time, and learns to determine the cause behind price motion, instead of waiting around for another man to do it for you.

Yesterday: There is nothing new under the sun. The mathematical student learns best from that, which came before.

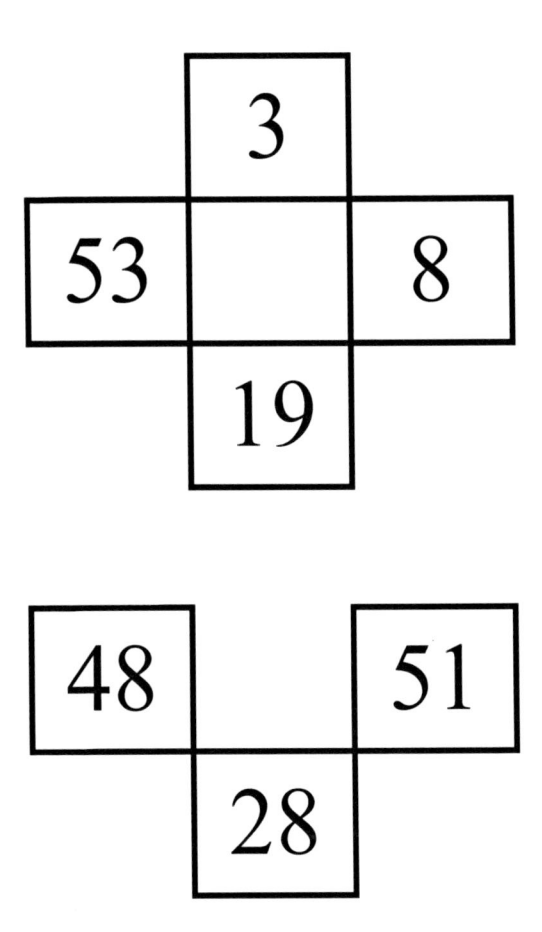

As A Stock or Commodity
Thinketh In Its Heart So It Is

	3	
53		8
	19	

| 48 | | 51 |
| | 28 | |

"In the beginning God created the heaven and the earth"

**As A Stock or Commodity
Thinketh In Its Heart So It Is**

Further Reading

The following bible verses are herein placed for the benefit of the reader who wishes to delve deeper into the mysteries of price movement as witnessed in the stock and commodity markets. To every reference listed there if a purpose and a use to the investor; and the best tools I would recommend utilizing are those of: the imagination; of reason and of mathematics.

Genesis 7:4	Mark 1:13
Genesis 7:12	Luke 4:2
Genesis 7:17	John 2:20
Genesis 8:6	Acts 1:3
Genesis 50:3	
Exodus 24:18	Genesis 1:11
Exodus 34:28	Genesis 1:12
Numbers 13:25	Genesis 1:29
Numbers 14:34	Genesis 3:15
Deuteronomy 9:9	Genesis 4:25
Deuteronomy 9:11	Genesis 7:3
Deuteronomy 9:18	Genesis 9:9
Deuteronomy 9:25	Genesis 12:7
Deuteronomy 10:10	Genesis 13:15
Judges 8:28	Genesis 13:16
1 Samuel 17:16	Genesis 15:3
1 Kings 2:11	Genesis 15:5
1 Kings 19:8	Genesis 15:13
Ezekiel 4:6	Genesis 15:18
Jonah 3:4	Genesis 16:10
Matthew 4:2	Genesis 17:7

As A Stock or Commodity
Thinketh In Its Heart So It Is

Genesis 17:8	Exodus 30:21
Genesis 17:9	Exodus 32:13
Genesis 17:10	Exodus 33:1
Genesis 17:12	Leviticus 11:37
Genesis 17:19	Leviticus 11:38
Genesis 19:32	Leviticus 12:2
Genesis 19:34	Leviticus 15:16
Genesis 21:12	Leviticus 15:17
Genesis 21:13	Leviticus 15:18
Genesis 22:17	Leviticus 15:32
Genesis 22:18	Leviticus 18:21
Genesis 24:7	Leviticus 19:19
Genesis 24:60	Leviticus 20:2
Genesis 26:3	Leviticus 20:3
Genesis 26:4	Leviticus 20:4
Genesis 26:24	Leviticus 21:15
Genesis 28:4	Leviticus 21:17
Genesis 28:13	Leviticus 21:21
Genesis 28:14	Leviticus 22:3
Genesis 32:12	Leviticus 22:4
Genesis 35:12	Leviticus 26:16
Genesis 38:8	Leviticus 27:16
Genesis 38:9	Leviticus 27:30
Genesis 46:6	Numbers 5:28
Genesis 46:7	Numbers 11:7
Genesis 47:19	Numbers 14:24
Genesis 47:23	Numbers 16:40
Genesis 47:24	Numbers 18:19
Genesis 48:4	Numbers 20:5
Genesis 48:11	Numbers 24:7
Genesis 48:19	Numbers 25:13
Exodus 16:31	Deuteronomy 1:8
Exodus 28:43	Deuteronomy 4:37

**As A Stock or Commodity
Thinketh In Its Heart So It Is**

Deuteronomy 10:15	Ezra 2:59
Deuteronomy 11:9	Ezra 9:2
Deuteronomy 11:10	Nehemiah 7:61
Deuteronomy 14:22	Nehemiah 9:2
Deuteronomy 22:9	Nehemiah 9:8
Deuteronomy 28:38	Esther 6:13
Deuteronomy 28:46	Esther 9:27
Deuteronomy 28:59	Esther 9:28
Deuteronomy 30:6	Esther 9:31
Deuteronomy 30:19	Esther 10:3
Deuteronomy 31:21	Job 5:25
Deuteronomy 34:4	Job 21:8
Joshua 24:3	Job 39:12
Ruth 4:12	Psalm 18:50
1 Samuel 2:20	Psalm 21:10
1 Samuel 8:15	Psalm 22:23
1 Samuel 20:42	Psalm 22:30
1 Samuel 24:21	Psalm 25:13
2 Samuel 4:8	Psalm 37:25
2 Samuel 7:12	Psalm 37:26
2 Samuel 22:51	Psalm 37:28
1 Kings 2:33	Psalm 69:36
1 Kings 11:14	Psalm 89:4
1 Kings 11:39	Psalm 89:29
1 Kings 18:32	Psalm 89:36
2 Kings 5:27	Psalm 102:28
2 Kings 11:1	Psalm 105:6
2 Kings 17:20	Psalm 106:27
2 Kings 25:25	Psalm 112:2
1 Chronicles 16:13	Psalm 126:6
1 Chronicles 17:11	Proverbs 11:21
2 Chronicles 20:7	Ecclesiastes 11:6
2 Chronicles 22:10	Isaiah 1:4

As A Stock or Commodity Thinketh In Its Heart So It Is

Isaiah 5:10
Isaiah 6:13
Isaiah 14:20
Isaiah 17:11
Isaiah 23:3
Isaiah 30:23
Isaiah 41:8
Isaiah 43:5
Isaiah 44:3
Isaiah 45:19
Isaiah 45:25
Isaiah 48:19
Isaiah 53:10
Isaiah 54:3
Isaiah 55:10
Isaiah 57:3
Isaiah 57:4
Isaiah 59:21
Isaiah 61:9
Isaiah 65:9
Isaiah 65:23
Isaiah 66:22
Jeremiah 2:21
Jeremiah 7:15
Jeremiah 22:28
Jeremiah 22:30
Jeremiah 23:8
Jeremiah 29:32
Jeremiah 30:10
Jeremiah 31:27
Jeremiah 31:36
Jeremiah 31:37
Jeremiah 33:22

Jeremiah 33:26
Jeremiah 35:7
Jeremiah 35:9
Jeremiah 36:31
Jeremiah 41:1
Jeremiah 46:27
Jeremiah 49:10
Ezekiel 17:5
Ezekiel 17:13
Ezekiel 20:5
Ezekiel 43:19
Ezekiel 44:22
Daniel 1:3
Daniel 2:43
Daniel 9:1
Joel 1:17
Amos 9:13
Haggai 2:19
Zechariah 8:12
Malachi 2:3
Malachi 2:15
Matthew 13:19
Matthew 13:20
Matthew 13:22
Matthew 13:23
Matthew 13:24
Matthew 13:27
Matthew 13:31
Matthew 13:37
Matthew 13:38
Matthew 17:20
Matthew 22:24
Mark 4:26

As A Stock or Commodity Thinketh In Its Heart So It Is

Mark 4:27	2 Timothy 2:8
Mark 4:31	Hebrews 2:16
Mark 12:19	Hebrews 11:11
Mark 12:20	Hebrews 11:18
Mark 12:21	1 Peter 1:23
Mark 12:22	1 John 3:9
Luke 1:55	Revelation 12:17
Luke 8:5	
Luke 8:11	Genesis 1:11
Luke 13:19	Genesis 1:12
Luke 17:6	Genesis 1:29
Luke 20:28	Genesis 3:2
John 7:42	Genesis 3:3
John 8:33	Genesis 3:6
John 8:37	Genesis 4:3
Acts 3:25	Genesis 30:2
Acts 7:5	Exodus 10:15
Acts 7:6	Exodus 21:22
Acts 13:23	Leviticus 19:23
Romans 1:3	Leviticus 19:24
Romans 4:13	Leviticus 19:25
Romans 4:16	Leviticus 23:39
Romans 4:18	Leviticus 25:3
Romans 9:7	Leviticus 25:19
Romans 9:8	Leviticus 25:21
Romans 9:29	Leviticus 25:22
Romans 11:1	Leviticus 26:4
1 Corinthians 15:38	Leviticus 27:30
2 Corinthians 9:10	Numbers 13:20
2 Corinthians 11:22	Numbers 13:26
Galatians 3:16	Numbers 13:27
Galatians 3:19	Deuteronomy 1:25
Galatians 3:29	Deuteronomy 7:13

As A Stock or Commodity Thinketh In Its Heart So It Is

Deuteronomy 11:17
Deuteronomy 22:9
Deuteronomy 26:2
Deuteronomy 28:4
Deuteronomy 28:11
Deuteronomy 28:18
Deuteronomy 28:33
Deuteronomy 28:40
Deuteronomy 28:42
Deuteronomy 28:51
Deuteronomy 28:53
Deuteronomy 30:9
Joshua 5:12
Judges 9:11
2 Samuel 16:2
2 Kings 19:30
Nehemiah 9:25
Nehemiah 9:36
Nehemiah 10:35
Nehemiah 10:37
Psalm 1:3
Psalm 21:10
Psalm 72:16
Psalm 92:14
Psalm 104:13
Psalm 105:35
Psalm 127:3
Psalm 132:11
Proverbs 1:31
Proverbs 8:19
Proverbs 10:16
Proverbs 11:30
Proverbs 12:12

Proverbs 12:14
Proverbs 13:2
Proverbs 18:20
Proverbs 18:21
Proverbs 27:18
Proverbs 31:16
Proverbs 31:31
Song of Solomon 2:3
Song of Solomon 8:11
Song of Solomon 8:12
Isaiah 3:10
Isaiah 4:2
Isaiah 10:12
Isaiah 13:18
Isaiah 14:29
Isaiah 27:6
Isaiah 27:9
Isaiah 28:4
Isaiah 37:30
Isaiah 37:31
Isaiah 57:19
Isaiah 65:21
Jeremiah 2:7
Jeremiah 6:19
Jeremiah 7:20
Jeremiah 11:16
Jeremiah 11:19
Jeremiah 12:2
Jeremiah 17:8
Jeremiah 17:10
Jeremiah 21:14
Jeremiah 29:5
Jeremiah 29:28

As A Stock or Commodity
Thinketh In Its Heart So It Is

Jeremiah 32:19	Malachi 1:12
Lamentations 2:20	Malachi 3:11
Ezekiel 17:8	Matthew 3:10
Ezekiel 17:9	Matthew 7:17
Ezekiel 17:23	Matthew 7:18
Ezekiel 19:12	Matthew 7:19
Ezekiel 19:14	Matthew 12:33
Ezekiel 25:4	Matthew 13:8
Ezekiel 34:27	Matthew 13:23
Ezekiel 36:8	Matthew 13:26
Ezekiel 36:11	Matthew 21:19
Ezekiel 36:30	Matthew 21:34
Ezekiel 47:12	Matthew 26:29
Daniel 4:12	Mark 4:7
Daniel 4:14	Mark 4:8
Daniel 4:21	Mark 4:20
Hosea 9:16	Mark 4:28
Hosea 10:1	Mark 4:29
Hosea 10:13	Mark 11:14
Hosea 14:8	Mark 12:2
Joel 2:22	Mark 14:25
Amos 2:9	Luke 1:42
Amos 6:12	Luke 3:9
Amos 7:14	Luke 6:43
Amos 8:1	Luke 6:44
Amos 8:2	Luke 8:8
Amos 9:14	Luke 8:14
Micah 6:7	Luke 8:15
Micah 7:1	Luke 13:6
Micah 7:13	Luke 13:7
Habakkuk 3:17	Luke 13:9
Haggai 1:10	Luke 20:10
Zechariah 8:12	Luke 22:18

As A Stock or Commodity
Thinketh In Its Heart So It Is

John 4:36
John 12:24
John 15:2
John 15:4
John 15:5
John 15:8
John 15:16
Acts 2:30
Romans 1:13
Romans 6:21
Romans 6:22
Romans 7:4
Romans 7:5
Romans 15:28
1 Corinthians 9:7
Galatians 5:22
Ephesians 5:9
Philippians 1:22
Philippians 4:17
Colossians 1:6
Hebrews 12:11
Hebrews 13:15
James 3:18
James 5:7
James 5:18
Jude 1:12
Revelation 22:2

Genesis 2:5
Exodus 15:17
Deuteronomy 16:21
Deuteronomy 28:30
Deuteronomy 28:39

2 Samuel 7:10
2 Kings 19:29
1 Chronicles 17:9
Job 14:9
Psalm 107:37
Ecclesiastes 3:2
Isaiah 5:7
Isaiah 17:10
Isaiah 17:11
Isaiah 37:30
Isaiah 41:19
Isaiah 51:16
Isaiah 53:2
Isaiah 65:21
Isaiah 65:22
Jeremiah 1:10
Jeremiah 2:21
Jeremiah 18:9
Jeremiah 24:6
Jeremiah 29:5
Jeremiah 29:28
Jeremiah 31:5
Jeremiah 31:28
Jeremiah 32:41
Jeremiah 35:7
Jeremiah 42:10
Ezekiel 17:22
Ezekiel 17:23
Ezekiel 28:26
Ezekiel 34:29
Ezekiel 36:36
Daniel 11:45
Amos 9:14

As A Stock or Commodity Thinketh In Its Heart So It Is

Amos 9:15
Zephaniah 1:13
Matthew 15:13

Genesis 8:22
Genesis 30:14
Genesis 45:6
Exodus 23:16
Exodus 34:21
Exodus 34:22
Leviticus 19:9
Leviticus 23:10
Leviticus 23:22
Leviticus 25:5
Deuteronomy 24:19
Joshua 3:15
Judges 15:1
Ruth 1:22
Ruth 2:21
Ruth 2:23
1 Samuel 6:13
1 Samuel 8:12
1 Samuel 12:17
2 Samuel 21:9
2 Samuel 21:10
2 Samuel 23:13
Job 5:5
Proverbs 6:8
Proverbs 10:5
Proverbs 20:4
Proverbs 25:13
Proverbs 26:1
Isaiah 9:3

Isaiah 16:9
Isaiah 17:11
Isaiah 18:4
Isaiah 18:5
Isaiah 23:3
Jeremiah 5:17
Jeremiah 5:24
Jeremiah 8:20
Jeremiah 50:16
Jeremiah 51:33
Hosea 6:11
Joel 1:11
Joel 3:13
Amos 4:7
Matthew 9:37
Matthew 9:38
Matthew 13:30
Matthew 13:39
Mark 4:29
Luke 10:2
John 4:35
Revelation 14:15

Genesis 11:30
Genesis 16:11
Genesis 17:10
Genesis 17:12
Genesis 17:14
Genesis 17:17
Genesis 18:13
Genesis 19:36
Genesis 21:8
Genesis 21:14

As A Stock or Commodity
Thinketh In Its Heart So It Is

Genesis 21:15	1 Samuel 2:18
Genesis 21:16	1 Samuel 2:21
Genesis 37:30	1 Samuel 2:26
Genesis 38:24	1 Samuel 3:1
Genesis 38:25	1 Samuel 3:8
Genesis 42:22	1 Samuel 4:19
Genesis 44:20	1 Samuel 4:21
Exodus 2:2	2 Samuel 6:23
Exodus 2:3	2 Samuel 11:5
Exodus 2:6	2 Samuel 12:14
Exodus 2:7	2 Samuel 12:15
Exodus 2:9	2 Samuel 12:16
Exodus 2:10	2 Samuel 12:18
Exodus 21:22	2 Samuel 12:19
Exodus 22:22	2 Samuel 12:21
Leviticus 12:2	2 Samuel 12:22
Leviticus 12:5	1 Kings 3:7
Leviticus 22:13	1 Kings 3:17
Numbers 11:12	1 Kings 3:19
Deuteronomy 25:5	1 Kings 3:20
Judges 11:34	1 Kings 3:21
Judges 13:5	1 Kings 3:25
Judges 13:7	1 Kings 3:26
Judges 13:8	1 Kings 3:27
Judges 13:12	1 Kings 11:17
Judges 13:24	1 Kings 13:2
Ruth 4:16	1 Kings 14:3
1 Samuel 1:11	1 Kings 14:12
1 Samuel 1:22	1 Kings 14:17
1 Samuel 1:24	1 Kings 17:21
1 Samuel 1:25	1 Kings 17:22
1 Samuel 1:27	1 Kings 17:23
1 Samuel 2:11	2 Kings 4:14

As A Stock or Commodity
Thinketh In Its Heart So It Is

2 Kings 4:18	Isaiah 26:18
2 Kings 4:26	Isaiah 49:15
2 Kings 4:29	Isaiah 54:1
2 Kings 4:30	Isaiah 65:20
2 Kings 4:31	Isaiah 66:7
2 Kings 4:32	Jeremiah 1:6
2 Kings 4:34	Jeremiah 1:7
2 Kings 4:35	Jeremiah 4:31
2 Kings 5:14	Jeremiah 20:15
2 Kings 8:12	Jeremiah 30:6
2 Kings 15:16	Jeremiah 31:8
Job 3:3	Jeremiah 31:20
Psalm 131:2	Jeremiah 44:7
Proverbs 20:11	Lamentations 4:4
Proverbs 22:6	Hosea 11:1
Proverbs 22:15	Hosea 13:16
Proverbs 23:13	Amos 1:13
Proverbs 23:24	Matthew 1:18
Proverbs 29:15	Matthew 1:23
Proverbs 29:21	Matthew 2:8
Ecclesiastes 4:8	Matthew 2:9
Ecclesiastes 4:13	Matthew 2:11
Ecclesiastes 4:15	Matthew 2:13
Ecclesiastes 10:16	Matthew 2:14
Ecclesiastes 11:5	Matthew 2:20
Isaiah 3:5	Matthew 2:21
Isaiah 7:16	Matthew 10:21
Isaiah 8:4	Matthew 17:18
Isaiah 9:6	Matthew 18:2
Isaiah 10:19	Matthew 18:4
Isaiah 11:6	Matthew 18:5
Isaiah 11:8	Matthew 23:15
Isaiah 26:17	Matthew 24:19

As A Stock or Commodity
Thinketh In Its Heart So It Is

Mark 9:21	1 Corinthians 13:11
Mark 9:24	Galatians 4:1
Mark 9:36	1 Thessalonians 5:3
Mark 10:15	2 Timothy 3:15
Mark 13:17	Hebrews 11:11
Luke 1:7	Hebrews 11:23
Luke 1:59	Revelation 12:2
Luke 1:66	Revelation 12:4
Luke 1:76	Revelation 12:5
Luke 1:80	Revelation 12:13
Luke 2:5	
Luke 2:17	2 Kings 14:25
Luke 2:21	Jonah 1:1
Luke 2:27	Jonah 1:3
Luke 2:34	Jonah 1:5
Luke 2:40	Jonah 1:7
Luke 2:43	Jonah 1:15
Luke 9:38	Jonah 1:17
Luke 9:42	Jonah 2:1
Luke 9:47	Jonah 2:10
Luke 9:48	Jonah 3:1
Luke 18:17	Jonah 3:3
Luke 21:23	Jonah 3:4
John 4:49	Jonah 4:1
John 16:21	Jonah 4:5
Acts 4:27	Jonah 4:6
Acts 4:30	Jonah 4:8
Acts 7:5	Jonah 4:9
Acts 13:10	

**As A Stock or Commodity
Thinketh In Its Heart So It Is**

Go to your bosom: Knock there, and ask your heart what it doth know.

As A Stock or Commodity
Thinketh In Its Heart So It Is

Index

A

ability, 4, 8, 14, 17, 24, 39, iv
absolute, 3, 4
accomplishment, 13, 26
action, 13, 22, 35
activities, 3, v
acts, 9
actual, 10
adhesive, 2
admittance, 23
adopting, 3
again, ix, 28, ii, vii
agricultural, 23
air, 23
alchemical, 6
algorithm, 26
altered, 8
ambitions, 11
annihilate, 3
announce, 2
anxious, 12
aphorism, 1
application, 3, iv, vi
architects, 4, 31
arithmetical, 19
armoury, 3
Art, viii, 2, 3, 4, 35, iii
ascend, 3
aspect, 7, 13
astrology, 23
atoms, 7
attain, 19, v
author, 10
authorities, 2

B

become, 2, 11, 12, 18, 19, 30, 33, 38, v
bitter, 1, 14
bloom, 30
body, 21, 22, 23
book, iii, viii, ix, 12
breaking, 1, 2
breath, 2
built, 2, 7, 32

C

cardioid, 22
cause, viii, 3, 4, 10, 11, 13, 16, 22, 25, 31, 35, 40, vii
chance, 7, vi
chaotic, 1, 27
character, ix, 1, 6, 7, 18, 28, 37, 38
chart, 6, 11, 18, 22, 24, ii, vi
chemical, 3
child, 3, 23
Childhood, 40
commodity, 1, 2, 3, 5, 6, 7, 8, 9, 10, 13, 18, 19, 21, 27, 29, 30, 33, 36, 37, 38, ii, iii, iv, vi
complete, 1
comprehend, ix, iv
connected, 7, 14
connection, viii, 4
consciously, 10, 14
consensus, 2
corn, 15

xxii

corrupt, 22
cultivated, 6
current, 4, 7, 8, 18
cycle, 2, 16, vi

D

daily, 3
day, 1, 17, 23, 25, 27, 31, 33, 34, iv
deceptive, 12
demand, 2
depression, 9, 18
descends, 16
desire, 13, 32, 37
destiny, 1, 4, 7
development, 7
diamonds, 4
dig, 4
direction, ix, 4, 14, 28, 40, ii
Disclosure, 40
distasteful, 3
divinity, 11
dreamers, 31
dreams, 9, 31, 33, ii

E

earnest, 3
earth, 23, 29
economic, viii, 1, 4, 8, 9, 19, 21, 36
effect, viii, 3, 4, 15, 17, 35
Egyptian, 3
element, 7
energy, 1, 3, 28, 30
entity, 8, 9, 21, 26
environment, ix, 7, 8, 9, 18, 19
evidence, 4

example, 4, 21
exchange, 8, 13
experience, viii, 4, 14
external, 4, 9, 10, 11, 13, 14, 16, 18

F

faces, 24
failure, 19, 27, 30
false, 19
fashion, 3
fear, 9, 18, 21, 30, ii
Fiction, ii
field, 26, ii
financial, ii
fire, 23, iv
fluctuations, ix, 6, 8, 10, 11, 13, 14, 24, 25, 35, 37
forces, 6, 27
forecasting, 15
Foreknowledge, viii, 3
forge, 3
frequency, 2, vi
fruitage, 1, 9, 37
future, ix, 2, 8, 11, 12, 14, 15, 17, 18, 22, 26, 28, 32, 33, 36, 39, 40

G

gamble, 2, 12
garden, 6
gold, 4, 37
growth, 3, 8, 40

H

hard, 14, 19
harmony, 7, 15

As A Stock or Commodity
Thinketh In Its Heart So It Is

health, 21
heart, 1, 5, 10, 12, 22, 27, 31, 32, 33
hidden, 8, 16, 39, iii
higher, 30
hole, 24
holy, 22, 27
hour, 10
human, 1, 3, 14, 20, 21, 23, 27, 33

I

ignorance, 11, 14
impure, 6, 14, 15, 18, 21, 22
indication, 7, 15, 35
individual, 3, 9, 13, 15
investigation, 4, 17
investor, 6, 7, 8, 9, 10, 11, 12, 13, 14, 15, 16, 17, 19, 21, 23, 24, 26, 27, 28, 29, 30, 31, 32, 33, 34, 35, 36, 37, 38, iv, v

J

Justice, 17

K

keynote, 16, iii
kingdom, 40
knocketh, 5
knowledge, 4, 12, 13, 14, 16, 28, 30, 31, 35, 37, 38, iii

L

language, 4, 8, 14, ii

law, 3, 4, 7, 10, 14, 15, 23, 34, 36, 40, iii, iv
layman, 2
learn, 3, 8, 19, 25, 26, 36, iii, vi
life, 1, 2, 7, 8, 13, 14, 17, 19, 22, 24, 29, 33, 38, 40, ii, iii, iv
light, 3, 11, 13, 14
love, 40

M

man, viii, 2, 4, 5, 8, 11, 12, 14, 18, 19, 23, 24, 26, 27, 29, 32, 36, 37, 38, 40, iv, v, vi, vii
manifest, 2, 7
manipulators, 17, 21
mankind, 4
market, 11, 12, 17, 19, 21, 22, 31, 36
markets, 6, 8, 12, 14, 17, 24, 28, 32
masses, 30
master, ix, 6, 7, 8
mathematical, 6, 13, 22, 31, 33, 34
mean, 7
mental, 3, 4, 8, 15
mind, viii, ix, 1, 2, 6, 14, 16, 21, 22, 23, 24, 27, 28, 29, 32, 35, 40, v, vi
molecules, 7
monetary, 4, 36, iv
money, 40
mood, 24
motion, 1, 10, 13, 16, 27, 34, 37, 40, ii, iii, iv, vii
mystery, 4, 33, iv

As A Stock or Commodity Thinketh In Its Heart So It Is

N

name, viii, 18
natural, ix, 14, 15, 37, vi
nature, 40
nectar, 9
negative, 3, 10, 11, 16
news, 2, 14, 16, 32, 33

O

offspring, 20
old, 8, 24
order, 2, 12, 30, 34, iii, vi
ordered, 1, 14

P

pain, 15, 18
patient, 4, 29, 35
patterns, 6, 11, 13, 15, 19, 22, 38, vi
people, viii, 9, 10, 36, 38, v
perfect, 17, 22, 29, 32
period, 16, 32, 36, v
personality, 3
perspective, viii, ix, 9, 24, 27, 29, vi
phase, 10, 40
pips, 1
plant, 1
political, 2
poor, 12, 19, v
positive, 3, 11
potential, 31
power, viii, 3, 28, 30, 31, 35, 36, 38
prayers, 11
predict, 11
predominant, 2, 4
prejudice, 4, iii
premeditated, 1
price, 1, 2, 4, 6, 7, 11, 18, 21, 22, 26, 30, 31, 32, 34, 35, 36, 37, 38, 40, ii, iii, iv, vi, vii, *See*
prison, 24
produce, 6, 15, 18, 22
profit, 7, 9, 14, 39, iii
profits, 9, 11, 12, 13, 15
progress, 16, 26
progression, 9
proportion, 8
prosperity, 3, 9, 18, v
prove, 4, 25, 31, 33, 40
pure, 6, 15, 22, 24, iii
purify, 15

Q

qualities, 3
Questions, v

R

radio, 2, 34
reader, viii, ix, 13, 40
reflection, 4
Reflection, vi
rich, 12
rise, 12, 16, 33
root, 9

S

scientific, 8, 9, 10, 13, 17, 24, 31, 34, 40
scientifically, viii, 7, 26
seasoned, 10, 24
seed, 1, 6, 9

As A Stock or Commodity Thinketh In Its Heart So It Is

seeketh, 4
selling, 9, 18
serenity, 23, 37
services, 4
shadows, 24
silence, 19, vi
similar, 10
slay, 30
soil, 8
soul, 4, 17, 23, 33, 38
sphere, 3
stocks, 6, 7, 8, 9, 10, 11, 13, 14, 15, 16, 17, 18, 19, 21, 22, 23, 24, 26, 27, 28, 29, 30, 31, 32, 33, 35, 36, 37, 38
strength, 10, 28, 33, 38
stress, 10
substantial, 2
suffering, 9, 15
sun, 24, vii
sweet, 1, 23, 24, 37, 38
swift, 9
swings, 12, 18

T

tales, 29
technology, 26
Thinketh, ii, iii, viii
time, ix, 7, 8, 11, 12, 13, 16, 18, 19, 22, 24, 26, 27, 30, 31, 32, 33, 34, 36, iv, vii
trader, 8, 11, 30
traders, 8, 26, 27, 29
train, 18
treatise, viii
trend, 10, 14, 15, 16

U

uncertainty, 2, 11, 24, 26
understand, viii, 2, 7, 8, 10, 12, 15, 22, 24, 30, 31, 40, vi
universal, 21, 22, 27
universe, vi

V

Valence, vii
vibration, 2, 11, iii
visible, 3, 30, 31
visually, 4

W

war, 18
watch, 4
water, 23
waves, 9, 13, 37
weakness, 10, 28
wealth, 3, 14, 19, 28, 37, ii, vii
weapons, 3
wise, 8, 16, 18, 19, 35, 38
within, ix, 1, 6, 7, 8, 15, 17, 18, 19, 26, 28, 32, 34, 35, 36, iii, v, vi
wonder, 4
word, 19, 22, 28
world, 3, 9, 15, 19, 25, 32, 36, iii, vii
writing, 24

As A Stock or Commodity
Thinketh In Its Heart So It Is

More From this Author

All books are Fine Leather Binding Limited Deluxe Editions (1440 copies); & signed by the author.

The Book of Impulse £1,440.00
Veiled book for scientific investors and traders looking to learn the way to forecast the prices of stocks and commodities.

Dictionary Of Thoughts (for Investors) £5,850.00
Straight forward dictionary with the most valuable thoughts and practical tools used in the creation of a long range stock market or commodity market forecast.

Nsingo's Business Ephemeris £1,560.00
High value ephemeris tailored specifically for the scientific investor and trader.

Nsingo's Market Blueprints Private Sale
Permanent Charts for S & P 100 Stocks for measuring the motion of price for selected stocks and/or commodities.

Heaven On Earth Private Sale
Map or Globe presenting the updated (2012) alignment of the Heavens and the Earth. Includes manual for practical use.

The publisher reserves the right to change the listed prices at his own discretion. Changes in price will be communicated to the buyer before any transaction is agreed. Please email publishing@nsingo.com for book enquiries & questions.
OR send mail Enquiries to:

Publishing, Nsingo & Company Ltd, 52 Mellis Avenue, Kew Riverside, London, United Kingdom
TW9 4BD